ADOPTION

WHAT DOES ADOPTED MEAN?

A YOUNG CHILD'S GUIDE TO ADOPTION

Written and created

by

Edith Nicholls

And with lots of help from me.

i

THIS BOOK BELONGS TO

ADOPTION

First published in 2005 by: Russell House Publishing Ltd., 4 St. George's House, Uplyme Road, Lyme Regis, Dorset DT7 3LS. Tel: 01297-443948. e-mail: help@russellhouse.co.uk. www.russellhouse.co.uk

© Edith A. Nicholls. The moral right of Edith A. Nicholls to be identified as the author of this work has been asserted by her in accordance with The Copyright, Designs and Patents Act 1988.

British Library Cataloguing-in-publication Data: A catalogue record of this book is available from the British Library.

ISBN: 1-903855-73-X

Printed by Alden Press, Oxford

ii

ADOPTION

WHAT DOES ADOPTED MEAN?

A Young Child's Guide to Adoption

AND WHERE TO FIND IT...

WHAT'S IN THIS BOOK . . . .

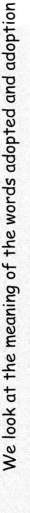
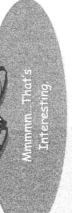

Mmmmm...That's Interesting.

ADOPTED—ADOPTION?

Just what do those words mean?

When we don't know what a word means we look it up in the dictionary and that says:-

Adopted—Taking another's child as one's own.

Adoption—Taking over from another person

Well, that's the meaning of the word. But what does adoption mean for you? In this book we are going to find out—so follow me through the pages and when you have finished the book you will know what Adoption means for you Then you can do the quiz at the end to see how much you have learnt.

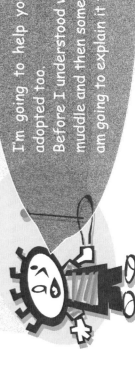

I'm going to help you through this book because I'm adopted too.
Before I understood what adopted means I was in a real muddle and then someone explained it to me in the way I am going to explain it to you through this book.

ABOUT THIS BOOK...

This book is about helping you understand what adoption means for you. This is your book and by the way, don't forget to put **your** name on the front of this book because it belongs to you.

I suppose there will be parts of this book that you may think are boring, boring (yawn, yawn) but everything in the book is important and you will see that when you come to the end.

Important things such as knowing about how hard it is to do all the right things for us children and why some born-to-parents are unable to do them. That part of the book will also help you understand why you don't live with your born-to-family.

Just remember, if there is anything you don't understand then don't keep quiet about it, tell someone and ask them to explain it to you again. Adoption is serious stuff! It's about you and your life and your future and so you should know what it all means for you.

Are you ready to go?
Well let's go!

LET'S START AT THE BEGINNING...

I suppose the first big question is -

Why is it that some of us don't live with our born-to-families and get adopted?.

Well, firstly, there are lots and lots of us children who have not been able to live with our born-to-families and have been adopted, and there will be many more in the future. We are not the only ones, there are loads of us!

And I suppose the next question is **What's a born-to-family?'.**

That's easy—the family we were born-to. Everyone has born-to-parents. Born-to-parents are the people who made us and their families are our born-to-family.
Who are your born-to-parents?

Born-to-mum

Born-to-dad

My born-to-parents are the people who made me. I call them my born-to's.

WHAT'S A BORN-TO-FAMILY?

WHY ARE SOME CHILDREN ADOPTED?

WHY ADOPTION?

It all boils down to what I call The Parent Thing.

You see, some born-to-parents are not able to do all the things a parent needs to do (that's all the stuff in The Parent Thing) to make sure we are safe, happy, well cared for and able to grow up to be healthy adults.

All of us children need someone to look after us until we are big enough to look after ourselves. If our born-to's can't do this then some one has to take over their job as a parent. That's adoption—taking over from someone else.

You see, being a parent is no easy job! There's loads of things to do, some are easier than others and some are really, really hard. And remember it's not just for a few hours or a few days—it's every hour of every day for a long, long time. And I know you'll understand this when I explain The Parent Thing.

But what you must remember, and this is important, just because our born-to's are unable to do all the things in The Parent Thing doesn't mean they don't love us, they do, they really do!

Things can get in a real tangle!!

9

THE PARENT THING...

Being a parent isn't just about making a baby, for some people that's the easy bit of The Parent Thing, although it is important and you will see why in a minute or two. This part is about making us and it comes naturally and we'll call it the **Born-to-Bit**.

Now the next part is probably the hardest bit to do and it has to be learned. This is the bit about how our born-to's look after us. It's about making sure we are safe and don't get hurt. I'm not talking about falling over and stuff like that but real bad hurt. It's about looking after us, caring for us, making us healthy and happy and helping us to grow up properly. We'll call this part the **Parenting-Bit**.

Then the other part is the bit that is up to the laws of the country we live in. There are lots of laws about how children should be treated and what parents can or cannot do. We'll call this part the **Legal-Bit**.

(Legal is another way of saying the law says it's right).

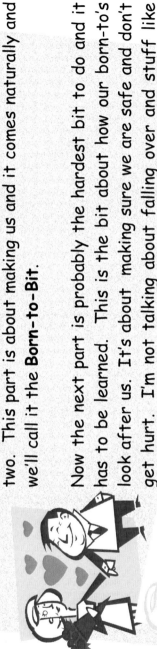

BEING A PARENT IS
NO EASY JOB!

THERE ARE 3 PARTS TO 'THE PARENT THING'

...AND ALL IT'S PARTS

I expect you are saying 'Ok, ok, but what has this got to do with my question about why some children are unable to live with their born-to-family and then get adopted?'. Well, I'm coming to that but it is important that you know just how hard it is for some born-to's to look after us even though they love us loads.

So now we know that there are three big parts to being a parent, in other words— three big bits to The Parent Thing, and they are:-

I got fed up at this part as well but it does get better honest!

THEY ARE ALL PART
OF
THE PARENT THING

BORN-TO-BIT

PARENTING-BIT

LEGAL- BIT

11

THE THREE PARTS....

As I said before being a parent or doing The Parent Thing is not always easy and for some born-to's it's really hard and no matter how they try they just can't seem to get it right.

Let's look at each part again:-

The Born-to-Bit = This comes naturally, most parents can do it easily and it's the bit that makes us.

The Parenting-Bit = This has to be learnt and is probably the hardest bit of all and it's about how we are cared for and looked after.

The Legal-Bit = This is the bit where parents have to do what the law says they should and can do for us.

IT'S LIKE JUGGLING

...OF THE PARENT THING

Now there is another thing you have to remember about The Parent Thing and that is that our born-to's have to do all the bits of it all at once. They don't do one bit then move on to another and then on to the next bit, it doesn't work like that. It's like trying to juggle and ride a skateboard at the same time, and you know how hard that would be.

Just telling you what the bits are doesn't really explain, you need to know what's in each bit to get a better picture of it all.

Would you like to see what's in each bit?

Let's go then...

THE BORN-TO-BIT....

BORN-TO-PARENTS

They gave us –

LIFE

The shape of our face, mouth and nose

The way we look

The sort of person we are—shy or outspoken

The colour of our skin, eyes and hair. Straight or curly hair.

THIS IS THE BIT THAT COMES NATURALLY

IT'S ALL IN THE GENES

....OF THE PARENT THING

Just look at all the things our 'born-to's give to us. Without them we just wouldn't be us, would we? They say it's all to do with something called 'genes' and not the sort you wear, that's jeans. These genes are something that's passed down through families and they make us what we are.

The size of our feet, hands and ears.

Our build, our height, our shape.

What illnesses we could get or might not get

How clever we could be

Our talents— art, music, sport

THE PARENTING-BIT...

Give us good food to help us grow

Love us no matter what we say or do

Help us with our school-work

Make us feel good about ourselves

Help us through problems or troubles

Keep us safe from any hurt or harm

Help us learn how to do new things

Take us to nursery or school when we are not old enough to go alone.

Show us how to look after ourselves

Now here's the hard bit

Take us to the doctors and dentist

THE BIT THAT HAS TO BE LEARNED

THERE'S A LOT TO DO

....OF THE PARENT THING

Give us hugs and cuddles

Give us clothes toys and books

Teach us what is right and what is wrong

Help us enjoy special days of celebration

Show us how to enjoy play and games

Give us a clean and decent home to live in

Show us how to care and look after others

Take us on holiday and days out

Keep us warm when it's cold

Take us out and show us different places

Look after us when we are ill

THE LEGAL-BIT...

Give us permission to stay over-night, or go on holiday, with friends and family.

Give permission for us to join the army, or the navy, or the air-force before we are 18

Give permission for us to get married before we are 18 years old.

Decide what names we should have and make sure our birth is registered.

Choose what religion they want us to follow.

Decide what needles (inoculations) we should have when we are babies

THIS BIT IS ABOUT THE LAWS OF YOUR COUNTRY

LEGAL MEANS THE LAW SAYS IT'S RIGHT

...OF THE PARENT THING

Give permission for us to go on school, or other groups, trips and days out.

Give permission for us to have an operation or have certain medical treatment.

Choose our schools and make sure that we go every day.

Talk to our teachers and decide what is best for our future.

These are all very important decisions about our lives and only our legal parents can make them. Born-to-mums are our legal parents the minute we are born. But not all born-to-dads are our legal parents, they have to be married or been married to our born-to-mums or given permission from a judge or registered our birth and have their name on our birth certificate, that is depending when you were born, to be our legal parent as well. If they are not our legal parent it doesn't mean they are not our born-to-dads it just means they can't make these decisions on their own.

SO THAT'S THE PARENT THING

It certainly is, and I told you there was a lot to it, didn't I? And what about that Parenting-Bit, WOW, there's loads to do and worry about, I get tired just think-ing about it!. Have another look at all the things parents have to do and then say what you think about it all.

I think...

Just imagine if you were not feeling too good, or had troubles and stuff it would be even harder to do all the things in the Parenting-Bit, wouldn't it? Well, you see that's what happened with our 'born-to's', it's true, honest, there are always reasons why some 'born-to's' can't do the Parenting-Bit'.

Don't believe me? O.K I'll show you on the next page...

WHAT I THINK ABOUT
THE PARENT THING

THE REASONS....

Not everyone's life is smooth and easy, some people have real troubles and things happen to them that make it hard for them to do what other people think they should. When it comes to doing the Parenting-Bit can you imagine just how hard that would be if your life was messed up?

Anyway I promised you the reasons why, so here they are:-

1. Born-to's may have troubles that makes it really, really hard for them to look after us properly.

2. Born-to's may have been shown the wrong way to do the Parenting-Bit

3. Born-to's may never have been taught how to do the Parenting-Bit

4. Born-to's may not be able to learn how to do the Parenting-Bit

5. Born-to's may be too ill to do the Parenting-Bit.

See, I told you there were reasons just like I told you our born-to's love us but you know loving someone is not enough, you have to do the things in the Parenting-Bit as well, otherwise we wouldn't grow up to be healthy and happy and we could get hurt.

Now I've got the reasons out of the way we can look at how we came to be living away from our born-to's and getting adopted.

LIVING AWAY FROM BORN-TO-FAMILY...

When our born-to's can't do the Parenting-Bit then we show signs of not being looked after properly. It could be that our nursery or school notice it or our doctor or other people in our born-to-family or even neighbours and even some-times the police get to know.

When people are worried about children not being looked after properly they let the **Social Services** know about it and they send a **social worker** to see us and our born-to's and to find out what is going on and to see if they can help.

I suppose you are asking the question:-

What is Social Services?

Social Services is part of the Local Authority, sometimes we call it the Council. Social Services have to help people who have troubles and the people who do this job are called social workers.

I remember this happening. Do you?

WHY I DON'T LIVE AT HOME.

WHY AND HOW DOES IT HAPPEN?

....AND HOW THIS HAPPENS

Where were we? Oh yes, I know, we were talking about social workers. They come to see if they can help but they also come to check if we are OK. Now there are a few things that could happen here.

If things are not that bad but they need to be better then the Social Worker will offer some help to make it better.

If things are really not that good but the Social Worker thinks they could get better then they'll ask our born-to's if they can look after us or in other words take us in care whilst they help our born-to's.

Now if our born-to's say no or if things are really bad and we are not safe then the social worker will go to a place called the **Court** and tell a person called a **Judge** about their worries for us and ask permission to look after us away from our born-to's.

Remember the Legal Bit and how it's only our Legal Parent who can make decisions about us?

GETTING PERMISSION...

Only our Legal Parents can say where we can or can't live and Social Services can't take us away from home without our legal parent's permission even if we are not safe. That's why they have to go to Court and see the judge to get permission. I'll explain on the next couple of pages...

ONLY OUR LEGAL PARENTS CAN SAY WHERE WE LIVE

THE LEGAL STUFF

COURTS, JUDGES AND WHAT THEY DO...

I know I've gone a bit off the track talking about the Court and judges and legal stuff but it's important to know.

Before it was all explained to me I was all muddled up but once I knew what this Judge person did I understood it much better.

The Court is a building where judges work. It's where all the stuff about the law is sorted out. It's a really busy place and there are all sorts of judges working there.

Some deal with people who have done things wrong and broken the law and some deal with things about children and their families.

The last one is the type of judge the social workers go to see.

THE COURT

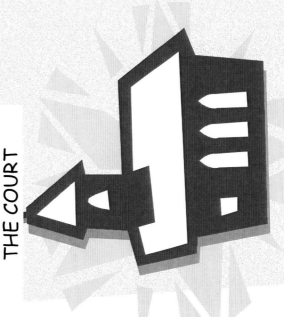

COURTS, JUDGES AND WHAT THEY DO...

Judges are very clever people and they know a lot about the law. They have to work very hard to be a judge and only the head of the country can say who will or who will not become judges.

Only a judge can make decisions about us and our futures without getting permission from our born-to's. They can make things called 'orders' and if people don't do what the judge orders them to do they could be in big trouble.

Some people think judges are all fuddy, duddy old men like him but they're not, they are really nice and when I got adopted I saw this really nice woman judge but I'll tell you about that later on.

When Social Services are worried about us and think it's not safe for us to live at home and our born-to's won't give permission for them to look after us then they ask the judge to give them permission to say where we should live.

THE LEGAL STUFF

A GUARDIAN IS THERE TO HELP US

Remember how judges are really clever people, well they don't just say yes to things without listening to what everyone has got to say, including our born-to's. Just to be on the safe side the judge will probably order Social Services to look after us while the judge gets a lot more information from all sorts of different people to see if Social Services were right and to see how we can get to go back home..

One of these people is called a **guardian**. A guardian is a social worker who doesn't work for Social Services but works for the judge. The guardian's job is to find out what we want and to see if Social Services are making the right decisions and then they go back and tell the judge. My guardian was great, she always listened to me.

Who is or was your guardian?

_____

Would you like to know how I came to be looked after by Social Services?

27

WHAT HAPPENED TO ME

I used to live with my born-to-mum and my 2 older sisters. I never knew my born-to-dad, he left us when I was a baby.

My born-to-mum didn't have a good time when she was a child and she never saw any of her own family. So she was on her own trying to look after us. She found it really hard 'cos some days she was sad and just didn't want to do any thing. She'd forget to give us our teas or not take us to school, and sometimes she would forget to come home at night and we were on our own.

Although sometimes we were hungry and frightened we loved our born-to-mum, still do, and didn't want to be anywhere else. We had a social worker who used to visit and try to help our born-to-mum and she would try but it only lasted a few days and then she'd get sad again.

Then my born-to-mum met this man, at first we all liked him and he made my born-to-mum feel happier. He used to bring us presents and sweets and when my born-to-mum said he was moving in with us we were all pleased. But that's when it all went wrong. He wasn't as nice as we thought, he used to hit my born-to-mum and she was frightened to tell him to leave.

Then one day he did something really bad and naughty to my oldest sister. We all knew, except my born-to-mum, but we couldn't tell the social worker 'cos he said it would get my born-to-mum in big trouble.

But my sister told her friend and her friend told her mum and her mum told Social Services and that's when it all happened. The police came and took the man away and the social workers took me and my sisters to a children's home. They'd been to see the judge and he gave them permission. I was 5 then.

We were all very sad and mixed up about what was happening. I know I was being naughty but I couldn't help it 'cos my head was in a muddle. Then my social worker said I was going to live with a foster carer and my sisters would be staying in the children's home. I was really scared, I didn't know what a foster carer was and thought it was a punishment for being naughty.

On the day my social worker came to take me to the foster carer I wanted to cry and cry, my sisters did. But I wasn't going to show them I was scared and instead of crying I kicked and bit everyone I could, it was awful.

THIS HAPPENED TO ME ◀

I was really surprised when I got to the foster carers' home, it was all nice and cosy and they were really kind and friendly and I felt a bit better. They were a couple older than my born-to-mum and they had grown up children who didn't live with them but came to visit. I had my own bedroom, nice clothes, nice food and I was going to school and making friends but I still missed my family.

My foster carers explained a lot to me including what foster carers are and do. They're just ordinary people you know, but they know a lot about what we need and how to help us feel better and they are only looking after us whilst the Judge decides what should happen.

I used to see my sisters and my born-to-mum 3 times a week in a Family Centre, that was good, but sometimes my born-to-mum didn't come 'cos she wasn't very well. I still felt sad at times and I would go and play with my foster carers' dog and it made it feel better.

My head became less muddled and I started to understand things better thanks to my foster carers. They said it was OK to cry so I did and they would give me a cuddle, I had never had one of those before, they're really good.

When I was living with my foster carers I had to see different people who asked me a lot of questions about how I felt, what were my sisters like and what was it like at home with my born-to-mum.

At first I didn't want to talk about it 'cos no-one told me why I should. Then my foster carers told me it was to help the judge decide. After that I started to talk lots, if it's going to help the judge, I thought, then I should talk.

Then my Guardian came to see me and she told me she would tell the judge what I wanted, so I told her everything I was thinking about.

I saw this man they called a psychologist, they said he knew lots of things about why children behave in certain ways and could tell what was best for us. I liked him, we played lots of games and stuff, it was good fun with him.

This went on for a long time and I kept thinking 'When's this judge going to make up his mind?'

31

Then one day my social worker came to see me and told me the judge said I couldn't go home to my born-to-mum 'cos she wouldn't be able to look after me properly. I was so angry I wanted to go and tell that judge what I thought about him. Then she said I was going to get adopted, well that really mixed me up, I didn't know what adopted meant all I could think about was that I was going to leave my lovely foster home and I was really scared again.

My foster carers helped me to understand with a book just like this one and I said "OK then, I'll meet this adopter woman that wants to adopt me". I'm glad I did I liked her straight away, she says she loved me straight away! Soppy or what?

Even though I really wanted to go and live with my new mum it was hard leaving my foster carers, I know they were sad too but they didn't cry in front of me. I still keep in touch with my foster carers we write to each other now and then. My sisters were adopted too and they've got a new mum **and** a new dad, we see each other 4 times a year and that's good.

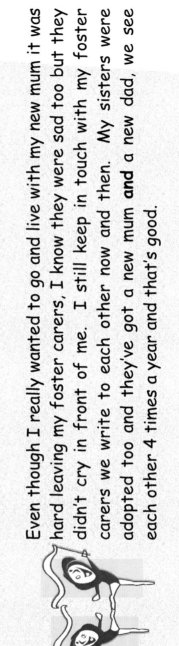

My born-to-mum is getting help not to feel so sad and I'll tell you more later.

So that's my story and all of us have different ones to tell like my friend here,

she's adopted too but she didn't really know her born-to-mum and dad because she was a baby when she was adopted. But she knows all about her born-to-family and every year she gets a letter from them and she sends them one back.

Maybe you should ask your social worker or your new family to write down what happened to you and why you were adopted.

All this writing down of stuff is called information and it really helps to know it. The judge used information to help him decide what was best for me and now I know why it took the time it did because the judge had to have information and loads of it..

33

WHAT'S THIS INFORMATION...

It's information about why Social Services think we are not safe at home. When I say safe I don't just mean getting hurt, I mean safe from any kind of harm, the kind of harm that can happen when born-to's don't do the Parenting-Bit. It's also information about what Social Services are doing to help born-to's do the Parenting-Bit so we **can** live at home, that's really important.

The judge asks all sorts of people for reports and this can take quite a while because it has to be done properly. Some of these people are what's called **experts** on things to do with children. That means they know a lot about what we need to help us grow up happy and healthy and some of the people know a lot about the laws on children.

And then, of-course, there is our born-to's. The judge listens very carefully to what they have to say.

INFORMATION AND LOTS OF REPORTS

IT ALL TAKES TIME

...AND WHY IS IT IMPORTANT?

It all takes time and it's not as fast as this rocket although sometimes you wish it was. There are times when you get all muddled because you don't know what's going on. I was like that until I realised that I needed to tell people how I was feeling, then I got answers and I felt better! Let's see who are the people and experts who helped the Judge know what was best for you...

THE JUDGE, THE PEOPLE...

The name of the judge _____

What they do or what they are	Their names
My Social Worker	
My Adoption Social Worker	
My Guardian	
My Psychologist	
My Doctor	
My Solicitor	
My Barrister	
My Foster Carers	

HELPING THE JUDGE TO HELP ME

EVERYONE HELPED THE JUDGE

...AND THE EXPERTS

Their names	What they do or what they are

You add in any other others

YOUR FEELINGS...

Phew!!! Isn't there just a lot to take in—time for a break and to think about what you are feeling and what questions you have. Feelings are about something we can't explain, like when the light goes off at bedtime and it just doesn't feel the same as when it's on. You don't know why—it just happens. How are you feeling now?

▶ WHAT'S IN MY HEAD AND IN MY HEART

HOW ABOUT SOME ANSWERS!

....AND QUESTIONS

And what about questions? You must have at least one if not trillions!

Ask your social worker, foster carer or new family for some answers.

THE JUDGE DECIDES…

So the judge has decided that the best thing for your future is that you have a new family to look after you, in other words—you should be adopted. (I know that because you are reading this book). That means you will become part of a different family and you won't live with your born-to-family. It doesn't mean that you should forget your born-to-family because they will always be a part of you. Remember the Born-to-Bit and all the things your born-to's gave to you to make you what you are? Well, that will never go away— come rain or come shine.

Now the judge will have given reasons for the decision that you should be adopted so you should ask your social worker what they are and write them down here, that's what I did!

IT'S THE BIG DECISION TIME

FINDING A FAMILY

WHAT HAPPENS NEXT....

Well now the people who are looking after you have to work really hard to find the best family for you to live with and to adopt you. And I don't mean your foster carers or the staff in the children's home, I mean the local authority or agency that have to make sure you are looked after properly.

They ask lots of different people who know you what they think you need to make you feel happy then they start searching for the right family for you.

They also ask our born-to's what kind of family they want us to have and what things are important to them, like religion or the way we live.

They try to find a family that will understand everything about us like our race, our education, our health and if we need to keep in touch with our born-to-family.

They look all over the place, North, South, East and West.

CHOOSING A FAMILY

They don't just take the first family that comes along. Oh no! The family they choose for us is hand picked to make sure they can look after us and love us and help us be happy and healthy. They're called adopters you know.

NEXT PLEASE...

FAMILIES FOR CHILDREN

THEY'RE CALLED ADOPTERS

ADOPTERS ARE ALL SORTS OF PEOPLE

WHAT'S AN ADOPTER?

That's easy to answer—an adopter is someone who wants to adopt a child or children. But you probably want to know who they are and how they come to be adopters.

Adopters are all sorts of different people— men, women couples, families. Some are married, some are single (that means not married), some don't have children and some do.

Before they can become an adopter they have to do all sorts of things like telling everything about themselves, learning all about what we need and how to look after us and being checked to see if they are good people.

They really put adopters through it because they have to make sure they are the best people to look after us. And there are other things they have to do as well.

FINDING FAMILIES

I know it's a lot for adopters to do, a bit like jumping through hoops! But that's better for us children 'cos we then know adopters are a bit special, and we deserve the best!

When they have told Social Services everything about themselves, been on training courses, been checked to see if they are good people and their family and friends have been asked what they think of them, the adoption social worker writes it all down in a report and that's read by this big group of expert people called a **Panel**.

Then they have to meet the Panel and answer questions. The Panel decides whether they are good enough to be adopters (it's called being approved) and then the Panel tells the head of the authority or agency what they think about them and then the head will or will not approve them.

Phew!! See what I mean—it's not easy to become an approved adopter.

IT'S NOT EASY TO BECOME AN ADOPTER

THE RIGHT ADOPTERS FOR YOU....

Now this is one of those important things again.

When people talk about families they nearly always think about a Mum and a Dad but families are all very different and there isn't always a Mum as well as a Dad or a Dad as well as a Mum. That's the same as adopters, they're all different too. Now it could be that the best adopter for you is a Mum on their own, like me, or a Dad on their own or it could even be different from that.

Let's make a big list of the different sorts of adopters who could be your new family—

1. A Mum and Dad who have children
2. A Mum and Dad who don't have children
3. A Mum on her own with no children
4. A Mum on her own with children
5. A Dad on his own with no children
6. A Dad on his own with children
7. A Mum who lives with another Mum with children
8. A Mum who lives with another Mum with no children
9. A Dad who lives with another Dad with children
10. A Dad who lives with another Dad with no children

THERE ARE DIFFERENT SORTS OF ADOPTERS

It's like opening a surprise present. You don't know what's inside but you know it will be really good!

WHAT KIND OF FAMILY DO YOU WANT?

When all the experts are choosing a family for you they will ask you what you want, so have a think about the sort of new family you want to be part of. It doesn't have to be what sort of adopter you want, it could be about where you want to live or what things you don't want or what you want to do when you have a new family.

I told my foster carer and my social worker what I wanted. They do try hard to get what we want but it can never be exactly what we want, but tell them anyway. I knew one little girl who asked for a mum with 2 telephones and she got one!

Make a list, it might help.

I want..... ....

....

....

....

WHAT I WANT

WHAT I WANT

MY KIND OF FAMILY

You don't have to feel as though you are floating in space all alone, there are lots of people you can talk to and say what you want, it really makes you feel better, you know. Why don't you try it and write down your wants and wishes.

x

47

MY CHOSEN ADOPTERS...

It could be that you already know who your adopter or adopters will be, you may have even met them by now. But even if you haven't this page is for when you have.

OK—spill the beans, let's have the info!

What are their names-

Where do they live -

What are they like -

MY NEW FAMILY

GOING OVER WHAT WE KNOW SO FAR

TIME FOR A RE-CAP...

That means going over things you know. Let's see what we know up to now...

The judge in the big Court building has decided you won't be able to live with your born-to-family.

The judge says that you should have a new family who will adopt you.

The judge has given reasons for this decision.

The local authority or agency that looks after you has to find you a family.

You can say what sort of family you would like.

You may already know the family that will adopt you.

Yes, done that. ✓
Yes, understand that. ✓
Yes, know that. ✓

A RE-CAP

WHO, WHAT, WHY, WHEN, HOW?

But supposing you don't know the family who is going to adopt you? You must have lots of questions like—

1. Who will they be?
2. How will I meet them?
3. What if I don't like them?
4. When do I go to live with them?
5. Why do they want to adopt me?
6. How long will it take?
7. How do I get adopted?

Well, let's carry on with the book and I'll try to answer these questions. But you may have other questions I haven't included. I know, before I try to answer the questions above why don't you write down your own questions and show them to your carer, or social worker or whoever is helping you with this book.

THERE ARE LOTS OF
QUESTIONS

I NEED SOME MORE ANSWERS

MY QUESTIONS

These are my questions...

Signed:

Date:

AND OTHER THINGS....

When Social Services were looking for a family for me I had a few worries. I worried about what my new family would be like, or if they would be the right family for me and or if they would like me. It was all a bit scary! Then I talked to my carers and my social worker and told them about my worries. They said I should write down what worried me or scared me.

My biggest worries are....

Try it yourself, it really helps and it makes the worry not so big.

MY BIGGEST, BIGGEST
WORRY

THEY CALL IT MATCHING

WHO WILL THEY BE?

Well I can't really answer this question exactly because your new family could be anyone but I do know they won't just be any old family, they will be carefully chosen especially for you. They call this **matching.**

Those expert people have to make sure that whoever they choose will be able to give you every thing you need to make you happy and that they will love you no matter what you do or say and they will keep you safe and help you grow up healthy and strong. Your new family will have to be able to understand what you need. They have to know the importance of your ethnicity and culture (that means the race of people you belong to and the way your born-to-family live their lives). They have to understand about your religion and what you need to keep in contact with your born-to-family, if that's what the Judge has ordered.

So I wouldn't worry too much about this 'cos it all works out OK in the end.

They'll be OK, just what you need.

HOW WILL I MEET THEM?

When your adopters have been chosen they will be given a photo of you and they will send a photo of them for you to see. You'll be told a bit about them to see if you like the sound of them.

If all that's OK then a meeting will be set up. It could be that they come to where you are living or you could meet in another place that everyone thinks is fine. Don't worry you won't be on your own, your carer or social worker will be there as well.

If that first meeting goes OK and you would like to get to know them better then they set up other meetings or visits to where they live or sometimes there are meetings when you go out with them. They're good you know 'cos they take you to places like McDonalds or KFC, or other places that us kids like to go to.

I don't know why my adopter wanted to meet me because the photo they gave her was the one I hate the most!

IT'S OK TO BE SCARED AT FIRST

WHAT IF I DON'T LIKE THEM?

Then you should tell someone, they want to know and they will help. But be careful that you are not getting muddled and you think you don't like them but it's really the feelings of being scared about it all. It's OK to be scared about it all, every-one feels a bit like that—including the grown ups. Yes, adopters get scared that you won't like them. It's really important that you talk about your feelings.

How I feel about my new family...

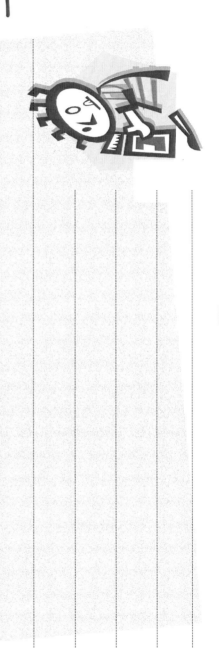

THOSE FIRST MEETINGS

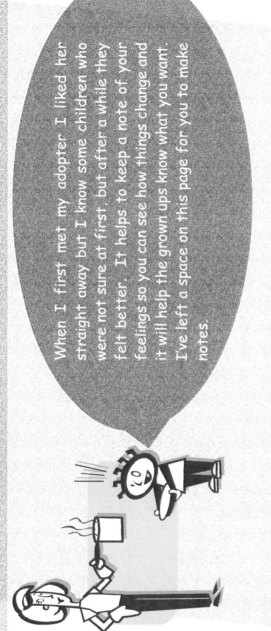

When I first met my adopter I liked her straight away but I know some children who were not sure at first, but after a while they felt better. It helps to keep a note of your feelings so you can see how things change and it will help the grown ups know what you want. I've left a space on this page for you to make notes.

IT CAN BE CONFUSING

GETTING TO KNOW EACH OTHER

WHEN DO I GO TO LIVE WITH THEM?

That depends on a lot of things but the biggest 'depend' of all is when *you* are ready to live with them. You see it's all about you and what is best for you. It can also depend on how old you are. The older you are the more time you may need to get to know them.

What the grown ups and those expert people do is get together and make a big plan of how you and the adopters can get to know each other better, they call this an **Introduction Programme.**

You go for visits, they take you out, sometimes you go for tea and sometimes you stay overnight or even a weekend. That way everyone can see if they are right for each other.

When you have an Introduction Programme get your carer to write it out for you and you can tick off the bits that are done.

MY INTRODUCTION PROGRAMME

DATE	WHAT'S GOING TO HAPPEN	✓ DONE

THE PLAN FOR ME

THE PLAN FOR ME

MY INTRODUCTION PROGRAMME

DATE	WHAT'S GOING TO HAPPEN	✓ DONE

Then that big day comes and you move in with them and live like lots of other families do, but you are not adopted when you move in, that comes later.

BUT WHY DO THEY WANT TO ADOPT ME?

This is a really, really good question and it's one of those important things again.

You see, adopters love their new children very, very much and they want to be able to do everything for them without anyone else telling them what they can or what they can't do. And that takes us back to that Parent Thing again.

When you go to live with them they are doing the Parenting-Bit (and they do this really well). They can't do the Born-to Bit only your born-to's can do that and that can never be taken away from them or you. So what bit is missing? Yes, that's right—the Legal-Bit.

Remember how your born-to's are your legal parents? Well they still are even though you are living with your adopters. Only a thing called an **Adoption Order** can make someone else your Legal Parent.

My adopter loves me loads and says I'm as sweet as a candy bar (soppy thing). She wants to do everything for me including the Legal Bit of The Parent Thing!

AN ADOPTION ORDER IS FOR LIFE

They want to be your legal parent so they can do all the things in the Legal-Bit. Things like deciding how and when you get your haircut to giving permission for you to join the army before you are 18. You remember them all don't you? Go back to page 18 if you need a reminder.

Now this is where the judge comes in again because it's only a judge who can decide who will be your legal parent. To make your adopters your legal parents a judge has to make what is called an Adoption Order.

Even though a judge said you should be adopted they don't do Adoption Orders there and then. That has to come later when your adopters have been found and you have lived with them for a bit, that's so you and everyone else are sure that your adopters are the right family for you.

That's another one of those important things because an Adoption Order is for life, it can't be undone. The only way an Adoption Order can be changed is by another Adoption Order.

61

HOW LONG WILL IT TAKE?

I suppose you mean when do you get adopted? Well that's another one of those 'it depends'. It depends on how long you have been living with your new family and how old you are, it depends on everyone feeling it is right to ask the judge to make an Adoption Order and then it depends on how quick the expert people get their reports to the judge for him to decide. And then it depends on when the judge has time to see you and your new family to make the order. So there are a lot of depends!

When you and everyone else are ready, your adopters fill in an application form to send to the judge. One of the questions on the form is about your names and what you will be called when you are adopted, 'cos when we get adopted we change our surname to our new family's surname. Some adopters give us an extra name to go with our born-to first names. The name may be a special name in their family.

What will be your full name when you get adopted?

YOU GET A NEW SURNAME WHEN YOU GET ADOPTED

HOW DO I GET ADOPTED?

THE JUDGE SIGNS THE ADOPTION ORDER

When the judge is ready to make your Adoption Order you'll be given a time and day to go to the Court Building. You go with your adopters and your social worker and other people from your new family, if they want to. When I got adopted we all got dressed up in our favourite best clothes, my new Mum looked lovely and when I told her she said I didn't look so bad myself!

They took us into this big room called a Courtroom and then the judge came in. I was really surprised when I saw my judge, it was this really nice woman. She smiled a lot and asked me to tell her who all the people were with me. Then she asked me a few questions, nothing hard, it wasn't a test or anything. She just asked what I liked doing, what's my favourite football team and easy things like that and then asked me if I wanted to be adopted by my new Mum. I said 'Yes' really loud and everyone laughed.

Then the judge said "Well, in that case, I think I should sign these papers". In other words she was making the **Adoption Order**! It was a great day, everyone was so happy especially me 'cos I finally got to be adopted.

YES

WHAT HAPPENS TO OUR BORN-TO'S?

Our born-to's will always be our born-to's but once we get adopted they're not our legal parents anymore and they can't do any of the things in the Legal-Bit.

The Social Services will try to help them, if they want help, they'll tell them about places they can go to meet other born-to's whose children have been adopted or talk to someone about how they feel.

I still see my born-to-mum, once every year. Me and my new mum go to meet her and I tell her all the things I've been doing. It's nice to see her and I feel better knowing she is OK, she likes seeing me too. This is called **direct contact**. I still love my born-to-mum but I love my new mum as well and everyone says it's just fine to love them both.

Remember my friend who was adopted when she was a baby and she writes to her born-to's and they write back every year. Well that's called **indirect contact**.

I saw my born-to-mum today

I wrote to mine last week.

KEEPING IN TOUCH WITH BORN-TO-FAMILY

HOW MUCH DO YOU KNOW?

SO DO YOU KNOW WHAT ADOPTED MEANS?

That's the question at the beginning of this book but I bet you know the answer now. Just to make sure we are going to have a fun quiz to see how much you really know—no cheating!

Just follow me.....

And me...

Who invited you?

You did! Remember - on page 33.

For the— MEGA ADOPTION QUIZ...

THE MEGA ADOPTION QUIZ

You get 1 point for every right answer so if you give 3 right answers to a question you will get 3 points. Get the picture? Next to each question is a page number, that's where you will find clues if you get stuck. Write your score in the box. There are 10 questions—have fun and good luck!

1. Name 3 things our born-to-parents give to us (Page 14/15)

2. Name 3 things parents should do to look after us (Page 16/17)

Keep going—turn over.

THE QUIZ

THE QUIZ

THE MEGA ADOPTION QUIZ

Hey, You're getting good at this

3. Name 3 things only our legal parents can do (Page 18/19)

4. Why are some of us unable to live with our born-to family? (Page 20/21)

5. Who decides if we should be adopted? (Page 40)

THE MEGA ADOPTION QUIZ

6. What are adopters? (Page 43)

I know the answer

☐

7. What's the plan called that helps us and our adopters get to know each other? (Page 57)

☐

8. Why do our new parents want to adopt us? (Page 61)

☐

THE QUIZ

THE QUIZ

THE MEGA ADOPTION QUIZ

9. When we get adopted what happens to our surname? (Page 62)

10. What does the judge have to make to make our new parents our legal parents? (Page 63)

Now get a grown up to mark your answers and add up your score.

How did you do? I bet you did really well. Let's go to the next page to see what your score means and just how well you really did. Can't wait.....

My final score =

THE RESULTS

If you scored between 8 and 10 then that's—Very Good

If you scored between 11 and 13 then that's—Excellent

If you scored 14 and over then that's—Super Duper Excellent

Well done! You must have been paying a lot of attention to this book to score so well.

What a result! But we haven't finished yet there's still a bit more to do.

MY SCORES

MY LISTS

Yes, that's right I want you to list all the things you think will be really cool about being adopted and you can also do a list about what would be uncool.

My Cool List

My Uncool List

FINDING OUT MORE...

You know it doesn't matter how much everyone tells us when we are getting adopted there will always be something else we want to know, and it might not be right now but some time in the future. So make a note here of who dealt with all the things to do with your adoption so you can get in touch with them if you need to...

The agency that looked after me was ....

The agency that dealt with my adoption was ....

Their address ....

Their telephone number ....
Their fax number ....
Their e-mail address ....
My Social Worker was ....
I was adopted on ....
My birth name was ....
The Court that dealt with my adoption was ....

GETTING MORE
INFORMATION

IF I NEEDHELP

GETTING HELP

Now there might be times when there are things that we adopteds start to think about and even worry about. This can happen even if we are really happy with our new families. It may be something we don't want to talk to our new family about or we may just want to talk to other children who have been adopted to see if they have the same thoughts.

Well, guess what, there are all sorts of different organisations out there that can help. If you feel that you don't want to talk to your new family about whatever is on your mind you can contact one of the organisations set up specially to help children who are adopted. I know a few but it depends where you live. Ask your social worker to write down your local ones on the next page. You can also look in the phone book or on the internet under Adoption or if that doesn't work ask someone you trust to help you or phone the agency that dealt with your adoption.

There is always someone willing to listen to you because you are **very important**.

WHERE TO GET HELP

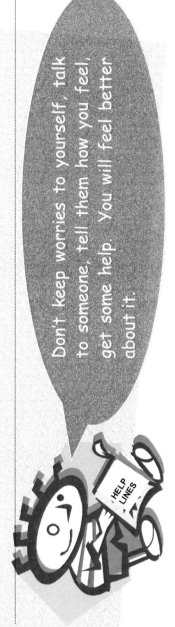

Don't keep worries to yourself, talk to someone, tell them how you feel, get some help. You will feel better about it.

HELP LINES

THEY ARE THERE TO HELP YOU

NOTES AND THOUGHTS

MY NOTES AND THOUGHTS

These are just a couple of blank pages for you to write down anything that you think is important about your adoption or your thoughts about this book and how it made you feel.

MY NOTES AND THOUGHTS

NOTES AND THOUGHTS

A POEM AND GOODBYE

THE END OF THIS BOOK

Well that's it, time to say goodbye. What do you think about poetry? I know it sounds a bit soppy but sometimes poets can say something in just 2 lines that would take me a whole book to explain. When I got adopted my social worker gave me these 2 lines from a poem by a man named Graham Greene -

"There is always one moment in childhood
When the door opens and let's the future In"*

Now isn't that just like being adopted? When you get adopted it's like the door to your future opening wide.

I hope your future is good and that you will be happy.

Bye, now, I've got to go 'cos I'm late for my guitar lesson, I could be famous one day!

* The Power and the Glory—1940

77

WHO WROTE THIS BOOK

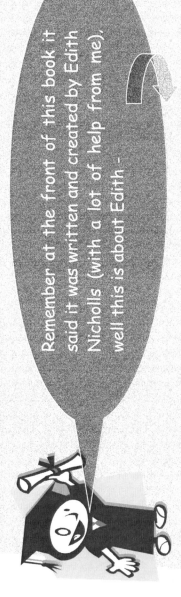

Remember at the front of this book it said it was written and created by Edith Nicholls (with a lot of help from me), well this is about Edith –

Edith is an adoption support social worker for Knowsley MBC (that's on Merseyside, close to Liverpool). She's been working in social work for over 24 years, phew, that's ages, she must be really old! She's done all sorts of different social work jobs like education, something called 'generic' work (whatever that means, the adults will know), child protection and has worked in adoption and fostering for 6 years.

You know she's even thought up this thing called The New Life Work Model and it's really good and it's to help all us children who are not able to live with our born-to-families. I like it a lot 'cos it keeps all our memories safe and tells us a lot about our born-to-families, cool or what?

What does adopted mean?
A young child's guide to adoption
By Edith Nicholls

Under the Adoption and Children Act 2002, all adoption agencies should provide adopted children, and children with a best interest decision of adoption, with a guide to adoption.

This unique, illustrated, interactive guide is for professionals and adoptive parents to provide information and explanation of why some children are unable to live with their birth families and the legal complexities of the process of adoption. It is aimed at *children under the age of 8 and older children with learning difficulties or conceptualisation problems.*

It is child friendly and uses age appropriate language to explain the complexities of the reasons for their separation from birth family and the decision for them to be adopted. It also encourages children to question, seek answers and reveal their wishes and feelings.

A cartoon character guides the child through various stages and talks with the child through the text. This character is a child who has been through the process of being looked after in temporary care, being placed for adoption and then adopted. His own experience uses a combination of a number of true cases in order to offer a wide spectrum of likely experiences, feelings and scenarios, and thereby to highlight significant issues.

This book can be fun as well as helpful with what children most want to know and what most concerns them. It helps children escape from feelings of blame and guilt, and includes what the author calls "a kind of reward section for the child with lots of praise". Adults who have to undertake the difficult task of explaining adoption matters to children will find the book surprisingly easy to use in the way it simplifies 'the telling' without diminishing it's importance.

ISBN 1-903855-73-X   Russell House Publishing Ltd., 4 St. George's House, Uplyme Road, Lyme Regis DT7 3LS

ADOPTION